TABLE OF CONTENTS

Cover illustration by
Tom Powers

Answer 17

Editor
Jeff O'Hare

Editorial Coordinator
Joan O'Donnell

Designer
Bob Feldgus

Graphics Assistants
Jason Thorne
Randy Llewellyn
David Justice

To order more copies of Puzzlemania® *SuperChallenge* books for young puzzle experts or for information about other products from Highlights® for Children, including the original Puzzlemania® book series for children ages six to twelve, please call **1-800-255-9517.**

1999 Boyds Mills Press
A Highlights Company
15 Church Street
Honesdale, Pennsylvania 18431
Printed in the United States of America

ISBN: 1-56397-792-3
10 9 8 7 6 5 4 3 2 1

WILD WORDS

What common word or phrase is represented by each of these word designs? For example, 4CHOON8 can be translated as *fortunate*. How many others can you figure out?

1. TROUi'mBLE

2. RISE
   IT
   N
   O
   T
   T
   U
   B

3. (see above)

4. MILK

5. CROSS / CROSS

6. ENDS
   ENDS

7. STAND
   I

8. THANK
   YOU

9. ⭐ 📺

Put wear and your long coat.

Answer 4

FRESH FOOD

Since our barbecue is just starting, we'd better make sure we have enough food. We made a list, but scrambled some of the letters. Can you rearrange the letters to find the names of food and drinks often served at picnics and barbecues?

1. GARRUMEBH _____

2. LETRPEZS _____

3. DMELNOAE _____

4. DUASRTM _____

5. MEICRACE _____

6. SHECEE _____

7. LKIPECS _____

8. SLORL _____

9. KOICEOS _____

10. ROOPPCN _____

On this list, we not only rearranged the letters, but we also lost a letter in each word. Can you add one letter and rearrange the new set of letters to find more picnic-food items?

1. DEAR _____

2. LADS _____

3. SHIP _____

4. PACTS _____

5. SHIRE _____

213

Illustrated by Cynthia Watts Clark

Answer 31

RAIN-FOREST RESCUE

This intrepid explorer is having some trouble in the rain forest. To help rescue him, figure out the correct order for these pictures. The only thing the explorer remembers is that scene D is where he started this trip.

324

WHAT AM I?

Start with 10 points. Deduct 1 point each time you go down to a new clue. See if you can guess what I am before the final clue.

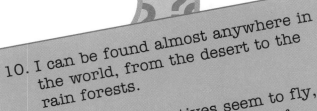

10. I can be found almost anywhere in the world, from the desert to the rain forests.

9. Some of my relatives seem to fly, though they really are gliding.

8. I am a mammal.

7. In cold climates, some of my relatives sleep through the winter.

6. I might be black, gray, or red.

5. I can be as small as a mouse or as big as a large cat.

4. I might live high in a tree, in among the rocks, or under the ground.

3. Prairie dogs and chipmunks are in my family.

2. I'm very thrifty and store food for future use.

1. I have a bushy tail.

435

Answer 9

There is one continent that has no native creatures of this sort. Can you guess which one?

COLOR BETWEEN THE LINES

Color the lines connecting each circle by using the fewest colors. No two lines of the same color can connect to any one circle.

546

SEW SIMPLE

There are 28 different types of fabric sewn into this grid in a unique pattern. Put each fabric in place by writing its name in the correct boxes. The number of letters in each word will help you figure out where the word belongs. You'll have this sewn up in no time.

3 LETTERS

NET

4 LETTERS

FELT
LACE
SILK
WOOL

5 LETTERS

CLOTH
DENIM
DRILL
LINEN
NYLON
ORLON
RAYON
SATIN
SERGE
SUEDE
TWEED

6 LETTERS

CALICO
CHINTZ
COTTON
DACRON
DAMASK
POPLIN

7 LETTERS

FLANNEL
LEATHER
TAFFETA
WORSTED

9 LETTERS

GABARDINE
POLYESTER

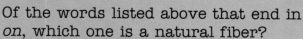

Of the words listed above that end in *on*, which one is a natural fiber?

657

10

'BOT-Y BUILDER

768

Congratulations! You have just been hired by Robocorp. You're a 'bot builder. And it's up to you to follow the clues and match the correct name to each robot.

1. Tinothy has three more arms than Gearheart.
2. The number of Tinothy's arms, divided by two, will tell you the number of eyes on Micah-chip.
3. The number of antennae on Cy equals the number of corners on his head.
4. Tinothy has two more eyes than Cy.
5. Gearheart has four more antennae and one more eye than Tinothy.

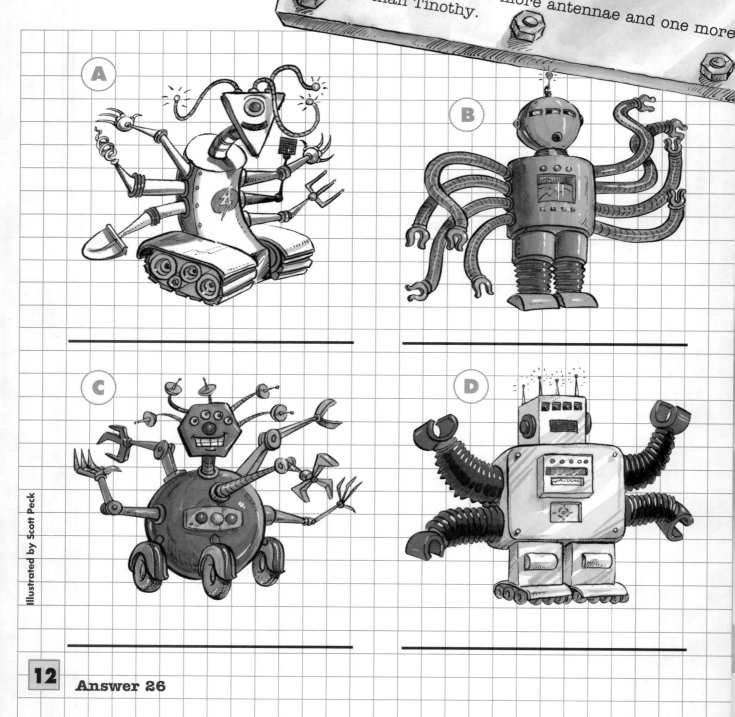

Illustrated by Scott Peck

12 **Answer 26**

WORD STRIPS

Each word or phrase below was torn from a list of other words. Unfortunately, part of the list blew away. From the fragments given, try to guess each word.

1.  thumbs

_____

2. sleeves

_____

3. artichokes

_____

4. unripe bananas

_____

5. pine trees

_____

6. shamrocks

_____

Can you tell what the items on the list all have in common?

879

Answer 16   13

GOING UP

Each of these five people wants to get off at a different floor. Can you tell which floor he or she wants to visit?

1. Miss Timmons wants to apply for a job.
2. Mrs. Olsen will get off at the floor directly after Mr. Burns.
3. Mr. Lang is going to buy a pair of earrings for his wife.
4. Ms. Murphy was the last one on and will be the first one off.

Illustrated by Scott Peck

6 PERSONNEL
5 TOYS, PETS
4 MEN'S CLOTHES ACCESSORIES
3 LINEN, JEWELRY HOUSEWARES
2 WOMEN'S CLOTHES ACCESSORIES
1 LOBBY

980

Use the clues to match each person with his or her name.

Answer 21

PLANTING ROWS

Read the first clue and fill in the word. Now remove one letter and rearrange the remaining letters to find the second word. Do the same for the third, then the fourth, fifth, sixth, and seventh. From the eighth clue on, add a new letter and rearrange the letters for the next word.

CLUES

1. A rabbit's favorite bunch of vegetables
2. Person in a play or film who acts along with the star
3. Way to cook meat
4. Heavenly body, like the sun
5. Sticky black substance
6. In the location of
7. First vowel in the alphabet
8. Indefinite article
9. Old horse
10. Pressed the doorbell
11. Liver, lung, or musical instrument
12. Moans in pain
13. Citrus fruits

. The first and last items have something in common. What is it?
. What four letters are shared by the first word and the last word? Rearrange these letters to form two new words.

201

Answer 5   Illustrated by Ben Mahan

15

SPARE PARTS

It's time for your yearly inspection. If you can identify an automobile part from each set of rebus pictures here, you'll be certified in no time.

312

Put this rebus puzzle together to get one more auto part.

lustrated by Lindy Burnett
hotograph by Peach Reynolds

JIGSAW JEST

Samantha was about to read the riddles of the day when her dog came in and tried to eat them! If you can help Sam fit the pieces back together, she'll recover the two riddles and the answers.

TEAR
A
-IER
KIND
RIPS
DOG
PAPER?
UP
WHAT
OF

423

-IER
CAN
PUT
RIPPED
TAPE
PAPER
TOGETHER?
KIND
A DOG
WHAT
OF
BACK
SCOTCH

I WAS THE FIRST

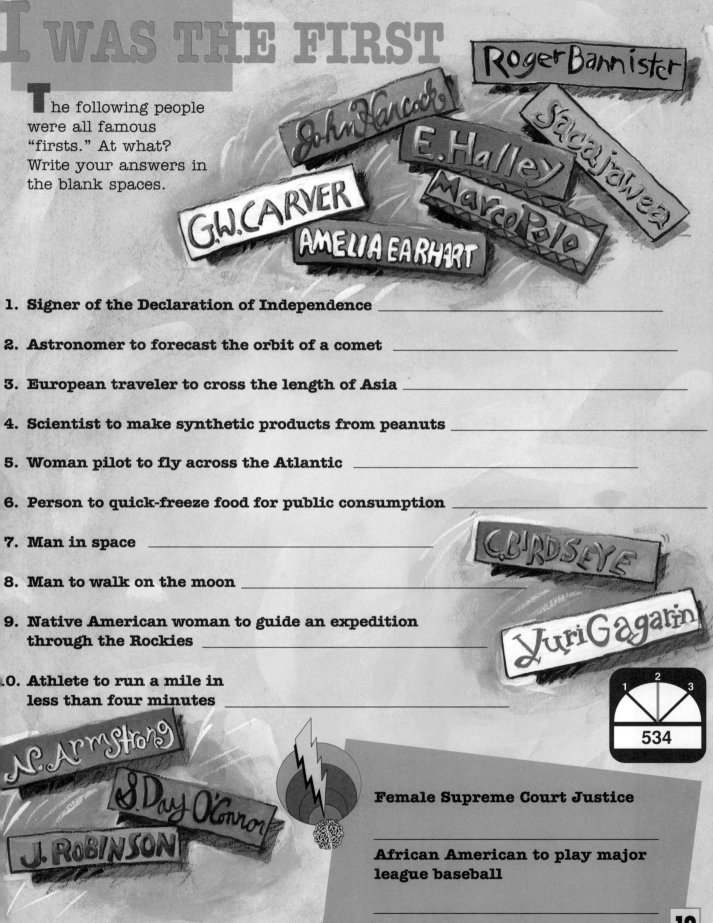

The following people were all famous "firsts." At what? Write your answers in the blank spaces.

1. **Signer of the Declaration of Independence** _____

2. **Astronomer to forecast the orbit of a comet** _____

3. **European traveler to cross the length of Asia** _____

4. **Scientist to make synthetic products from peanuts** _____

5. **Woman pilot to fly across the Atlantic** _____

6. **Person to quick-freeze food for public consumption** _____

7. **Man in space** _____

8. **Man to walk on the moon** _____

9. **Native American woman to guide an expedition through the Rockies** _____

10. **Athlete to run a mile in less than four minutes** _____

Female Supreme Court Justice

_____

African American to play major league baseball

_____

534

SURF'S UP

Write the answers to these clues in the correct boxes and you won't get wiped out.

ACROSS

1. Ship's steering gear
5. Unhappy
8. Opera solo
9. Weird or spooky
10. Pick up an object
11. Walk back and forth
12. Golf-ball holder
13. Desire
14. Sandy tanning spot
16. Moves up and down in the water, as on a fishing line
17. Electrical unit
20. Shelled sea creature
21. Actual, real
22. Deep holes in the ground
23. Snaky fish
24. American Medical Society (abbreviation)
25. Questions (verb)

DOWN

1. Stop
2. Canal near Buffalo, New York
3. Rescue crafts
4. Floor pad
5. Where water meets land (plural)
6. Curved structure
7. To color an object
9. Long poem or story
13. Existed, past tense of "is"
15. Recedes, like the tide
16. Hat border
18. Unseaworthy ship, or big brute
19. Chaos or clutter
20. Certified Public Accountant (abbreviation)
21. Drink served either hot or cold

Illustrated by Bradley Clark

TOOLS OF THE TRADE

Can you match each profession with the tools used to do the job?

Cobbler ——

Cooper ——

Orthodontist ——

Photographer ——

Glazier ——

Surveyor ——

Ophthalmologist ——

A
braces
pliers
molds

E
compass
tripod
plumb

F
lenses
film
light meter

B
glass
ruler
tape

C
staves
hoops
hammer

G
leather
hammer
last

D
lenses
eye drops
charts

Answer 2

1   2   3
756

TWISTED LOGIC

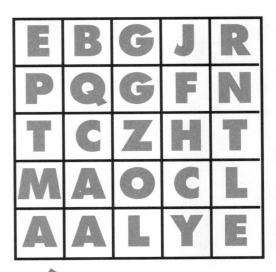

To find the name of a great snack food, use the grid and follow the directions. Write the letters you find in the numbered spaces below.

1. The first letter is the first of two letters that appear in consecutive alphabetical order, when you read from left to right.
2. The second letter is in the northeast corner, if south is the bottom of the page.
3. The third and sixth letters are in opposite corners.
4. The fourth letter appears twice in the third row.
5. The fifth letter is in the center.
6. See clue 3.
7. The seventh letter is the last one in the third column.

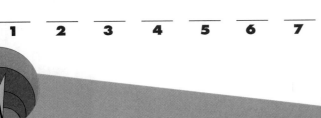

1 __ 2 __ 3 __ 4 __ 5 __ 6 __ 7 __

867

To discover in which country this snack was invented, use the grid again and follow these directions.

1. The first letter is above itself in the third column.
2. The second letter is the last letter in the grid.
3. The third letter is in the northeast corner.
4. The fourth letter is first in row 4.
5. The fifth letter is the letter that appears most often in the grid.
6. The sixth letter is the second down in the final column.
7. The seventh letter is at the bottom of the column that starts with J.

1 __ 2 __ 3 __ 4 __ 5 __ 6 __ 7 __

Answer 11

23

EGGSCRUCIATING

Don't be chicken. Gather up all the clues you need to decode these riddles. Each colored egg stands for the capital letter on the egg box. Match the eggs with the letters to solve the code.

A B C D E

F G H I J

K L M N O

P Q R S T

U V W X

Y Z

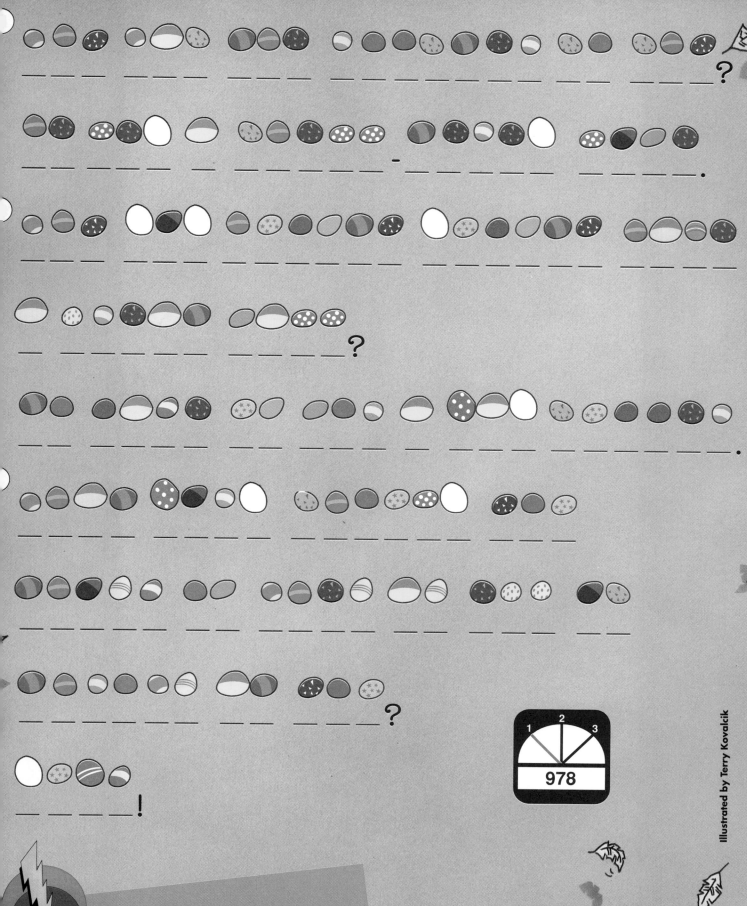

Name six creatures that are hatched from eggs.

Illustrated by Terry Kovalcik

ARROW HEADINGS

Start in the box with the S at the bottom left. Follow the arrows until you reach the finish at F. Once you start in the direction of an arrow, you must go on until another arrow allows you to change direction.

26

Illustrated by Steve Sack

Answer 15

TEAM SPIRIT

Do you know how many players a team can have on the field or the court at any one time in each sport listed below?

Football _____   Baseball _____

Basketball _____   Soccer _____

Hockey _____   Polo _____

Rugby _____   Cricket _____

Lacrosse _____   Bowling _____

Volleyball _____   Relay Race _____

The total number of players is _____.

Answer 3

Now see if you can divide the different sports into two columns so that the sum of each column is half the total above. Only the player totals must be equal in each column, not necessarily the number of teams.

_____ _____   _____ _____

_____ _____   _____ _____

_____ _____   _____ _____

_____ _____   _____ _____

_____ _____   _____ _____

_____ _____   _____ _____

Total _____   Total _____

1 2 3

244

MIND YOUR MANNERS

Sit up straight and follow the clues to find the letters that go in the numbered blanks. You will soon "Post" the answer to a riddle if you mind your manners.

- Letter 1 is on the spoon you should use for the first course.
- Letter 2 is on the plate that shows the customer is still eating.
- Letter 3 is on the napkin of the person who has left the table for a moment.
- The napkin that shows the person has finished the meal, including dessert, has letter 4.
- The knife used to spread butter has letter 5.
- Letter 6 is on the plate that shows another diner has finished that part of the meal.
- The water glass has letter 7.
- Look for letter 8 on the dessert spoon.

Why do new husbands have good manners?
Because they are

__ __ __ __ __ __ __ __ __ __ __
1   2   3   3   4   5   6   6   7   2   8

Do you know why we used the word *Post* in the introduction?

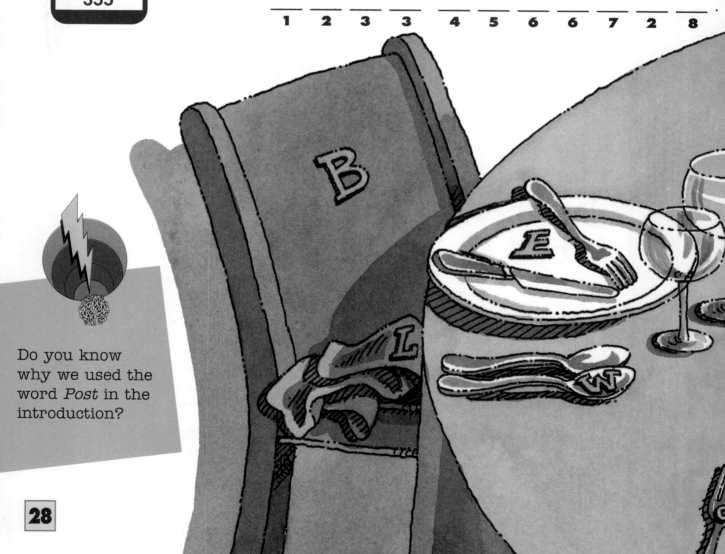

28

Illustrated by Laurie Hamilton

Answer 30

ADD IT UP

What could be easier than filling in a tic-tac-toe grid? Well, don't jump too quickly, because the numerals 1 through 9 need to be put into the spaces in a special order. We've included some equations to help you find the different numerals. When you work out the numbers in the equations, you'll know where to put them in the grid.

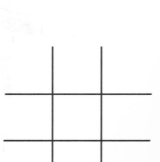

□ x □ = □

□ + □ = □

□ + □ = □

□ + □ = □

□ x □ = □

□ x □ = □

□ + □ + □ = □

□ x □ = □

□ + □ = □

466

Answer 7

KNOT LIKELY

The names of 15 different types of knots are tied up in this puzzle. See if you can untangle the mess by putting the knots in the correct spaces. Use the number of letters in each word to help you figure out where the word belongs.

ANCHOR BEND
ANGLERS
BARREL
CONSTRICTOR
FIGURE EIGHT

GRANNY
HONDA
MONKEY'S FIST
OVERHAND
REEF

SHEET BEND
SLIP
SQUARE
TAUT LINE HITCH
THUMB

Name two places where you might get a knot without tying or tangling anything together.

577

Photograph by Peach Reynolds

DUPLI-GRIDS

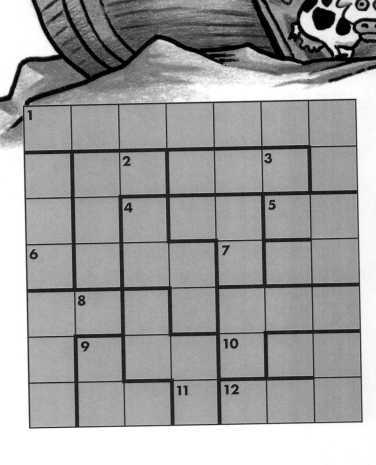

Here are two crosswords with a twist. The letters in both grids will be exactly the same. However, each puzzle has completely different clues and answers. Answer the clues in each puzzle without worrying about up or down. Place the words at odd angles to fit within the heavy lines. Each word begins in the box with the matching number.

LEFT GRID

1. Pachyderm
2. John, Jack, Sue, Amanda, etc.
3. Avoid this when eating
4. Large town
5. Dollars
6. Feline
7. Result of addition
8. Create a picture
9. Kitchen cookware
10. Extremely
11. Contact by phone
12. Get up

RIGHT GRID

1. It's filled with graphite
2. Chapeau or toque
3. Story
4. Not real
5. A lot of, too _____
6. Arrived
7. Take a break
8. Piece performed in a theater
9. Formal word to address a man
10. In the direction of
11. Hollow space in a mountain, or a bear's home

Illustrated by Steve Sack

Unscramble the four corner letters and the center letter to spell a word.

SHOPPING LIST

Each set of letters below can be turned into a word by putting the same letter in front and at the end of the word. When you complete all the words in each list, read down the letters you added to find something you might buy in a toy store.

1

___ a r ___
___ l e ___
___ u m ___

2

___ o m i ___
___ e f e ___
___ l p h ___
___ o l k ___
___ u t g ___
___ y l o ___
___ k i e ___

3

___ i g h ___
___ r a s ___
___ r i e ___
___ r e a ___
___ u m m ___
___ l u r ___
___ v a d ___
___ r o m ___
___ u m o ___

4

___ p i e ___
___ a y a ___
___ r o m ___
___ r e a ___
___ a g l ___
___ l u r ___
___ u t g ___
___ r e n ___
___ i v e ___
___ r i e ___

799

34   Answer 19

THREE IS A MATCH

Ten sets of three related words are hidden somewhere in this list of words. It's up to you to put each word in the correct category. Be careful, because many words might fit in more than one group. There's only one way to use all the words, putting three into each group.

Alberta	Fin	Scale
Bill	Flora	Shrub
Buck	Foreman	Stag
Burns	Georgia	Strap
Bush	Gill	Supervisor
Cash	Manager	Tail
Colorado	Manitoba	Tree
Crown	Martha	Utah
Doe	Ohio	Virginia
Fawn	Ontario	Washington

1. **Parts of a cap:** _____ _____ _____

2. **Names for money:** _____ _____ _____

3. **Bosses:** _____ _____ _____

4. **Names for deer:** _____ _____ _____

5. **Canadian Provinces:** _____ _____ _____

6. **People named George:** _____ _____ _____

7. **American States:** _____ _____ _____

8. **Female names:** _____ _____ _____

9. **Names for plants:** _____ _____ _____

10. **Parts of a fish:** _____ _____ _____

802

IF... THEN

Read each statement carefully. Follow our directions when our information is correct. When our information is incorrect, darken the box or boxes indicated. When you are done, you should be able to read an interesting quote and identify the person who said it.

1. If the word "handkerchief" is spelled correctly, place an I in boxes 1, 5, 9, 13, 21, 54, and 59.

2. If 67 multiplied by 35 equals 2,345, place a T in boxes 8, 26, 29, 31, 51, and 57.

3. If you should remain close to the ground when escaping from a fire, place a B in box 48.

4. If 486 divided by 27 equals 17, place a K in boxes 12 and 52.

5. If "thankful" is a synonym for "grateful," put a K in box 36.

6. If the speed of light is faster than the speed of sound, place a D in box 42.

7. If hurricanes begin on land and move to water, place a W in box 35.

8. If the word "habitat" is spelled correctly, put an S in boxes 14 and 56.

9. If "humiliate" is an antonym for "praise," place a W in box 39.

10. If the digit 8 is in the ten-thousands place in the numeral 428,457, then place an R in box 30.

11. If a complex problem is easy to solve, place a V in box 45.

12. If toxic waste is hazardous, put an N in boxes 6, 11, 28, 34, 37, 55, and 60.

13. If gasoline is flammable, put an L in boxes 40 and 47.

14. If the Pacific Ocean is the largest ocean, put a P in box 23.

15. If the sun is the closest star to Earth, place a G in boxes 4 and 43.

131

16. If it is earlier in Denver, Colorado, than it is in New York City, place an H in box 32.

17. If 0 degrees longitude is called the Prime Meridian, put an A in boxes 3, 7, 27, 33, and 46.

18. If 487 plus 867 plus 239 equals 1,593, place an M in boxes 2, 16, and 22.

19. If the word "misspelled" is spelled correctly, place an O in boxes 10, 17, 24, and 38.

20. If Pittsburgh is the capital of Pennsylvania, put a Y in box 20.

21. If Gaelic is a language spoken in Ireland, place an R in boxes 18, 25, and 50.

22. If a mushroom is a fruit, put a J in box 15.

23. If 12:00 noon is still in the a.m., place an E in all the remaining boxes.

1	2	3	4	5
6	7	8	9	10
11	12	13	14	15
16	17	18	19	20
21	22	23	24	25
26	27	28	29	30
31	32	33	34	35
36	37	38	39	40
41	42	43	44	45
46	47	48	49	50
51	52	53	54	55
56	57	58	59	60

Illustrated by Laurie Hamilton

Answer 10

SHORT STUFF

You'll be surprised at how much can fit into this crossword puzzle if you use the abbreviations for a lot of the longer words. An asterisk (*) next to a word clue means that you should write an abbreviation or a short form of that word in the grid. When a clue is already an abbreviation, you should write the word. Otherwise, this is solved like a regular crossword. You should be finished shortly.

ACROSS

1. September *
4. Ensign *
5. Colorado *
9. Ft.
11. Reef material, or pinkish color
12. National Broadcasting Corporation *
14. Massachusetts *
15. Medical doctor *
16. Irish short form of "father"
17. Federal Aviation Administration *
19. Mjr.
21. Word of respect to a man
22. Cash on delivery *
23. Video cassette recorder *
24. Scholastic Aptitude Test *
26. International *
28. Physical education *
30. Medical *
32. District of Columbia *
34. Charge *
36. Volunteer *
38. Grand Old Party *
39. Estimate *
40. Route *
41. Famous Texas landmark
43. Ampere (unit of power) *
45. South America *
46. A short laugh
48. Parent-Teacher Associations *
50. Issue *
52. One of the short forms of Elizabeth
54. Type of weevil that feeds on cotton
56. Michigan *
57. Federal Communications Commission *
58. Christmas *

Illustrated by Jim Paillot

1		2	3		4				5	6	7	8
		9		10			11					
12	13		14								15	
			16					17		18		
19		20			21				22			
23			24	25			26	27				
28		29		30		31				32	33	
	34		35		36		37		38			
39			40			41	42					
	43	44				45						
46	47			48		49			50		51	
52	53				54		55					
56			57				58					

DOWN

1. Sunday *
2. Private First Class *
3. Toward *
4. Estimated time of arrival *
5. Carbonated beverage
6. Oregon *
7. Los Angeles Municipal *
8. Not new
10. Belonging to someone named Omar
13. A support to keep a wall or beam in place
16. First note of the singing scale
17. Friday *

18. A major section of a play
19. Most valuable player *
20. Junior *
21. Stephen *
25. Ante Meridiem * (before noon)
27. New Orleans *
29. Ohio *
31. Director of Operations *
32. Type of stadiums housing Houston and Seattle sports centers
33. Chief Petty Officer *
34. Chicago Transit Authority *

35. Group *
37. Cowboy's rope
38. Georgia *
42. Louisiana *
44. Mobile Army Surgical Hospital *
46. Stitched edge of a dress
47. Allison *
49. American Broadcasting Company *
50. Industrial Light and Magic *
51. Distress call *
53. Intensive care *
55. Roman numerals for 60

FAMOUS MEN

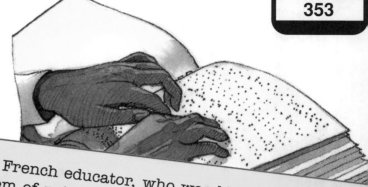

To solve this puzzle, write the answer to each clue in the spaces provided. Each answer will be a famous last name. Then decipher the message on the next page by writing in the letter that corresponds to each number. When you're done, you'll be able to read a quote from Sir Francis Bacon.

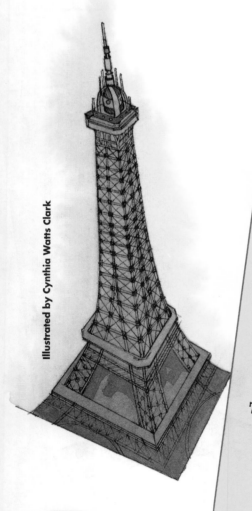

Illustrated by Cynthia Watts Clark

1. This French educator, who was blind, devised a system of printing and writing for people who are visually impaired.

— — — — — — —
  1   2   3

2. This code, which uses dots and dashes or short and long sounds or flashes of light, is named after the inventor of the telegraph.

— — — — —
4   5   6

3. This French engineer designed a 984-foot-high tower in Paris, which was built for the 1889 Centennial Exposition.

— — — — — —
7   8

4. This French chemist and bacteriologist discovered how to kill germs in milk and other food.

— — — — — — —
9   10   11

5. This man was known for his love of studying and sketching the different species of American birds.

— — — — — — —
  12 13   14

6. This scale, used to measure temperature, is named after the German physicist who devised it.

— — — — — — — — —
      15

7. These two men led the expedition that explored the country northwest of the Mississippi River in the early 1800s.

— — — — — — and — — — — — —
      16   17

$$\overline{}_{10} \quad \overline{}_{16} \quad \overline{}_{2} \quad \overline{}_{6} \quad \overline{}_{7} \quad \overline{}_{4} \quad \overline{}_{10} \quad \overline{}_{14} \quad \overline{}_{16} \quad \overline{}_{2} \quad \overline{}_{3} \quad \overline{}_{3}$$

$$\overline{}_{4} \quad \overline{}_{10} \quad \overline{}_{17} \quad \overline{}_{7} \quad \overline{}_{4} \quad \overline{}_{5} \quad \overline{}_{1} \quad \overline{}_{7}$$

$$\overline{}_{5} \quad \overline{}_{9} \quad \overline{}_{9} \quad \overline{}_{5} \quad \overline{}_{1} \quad \overline{}_{11} \quad \overline{}_{12} \quad \overline{}_{14} \quad \overline{}_{2} \quad \overline{}_{11} \quad \overline{}_{2} \quad \overline{}_{7} \quad \overline{}_{6}$$

$$\overline{}_{11} \quad \overline{}_{15} \quad \overline{}_{10} \quad \overline{}_{14} \quad \overline{}_{15} \quad \overline{}_{7} \quad \overline{}_{8} \quad \overline{}_{2} \quad \overline{}_{14} \quad \overline{}_{13} \quad \overline{}_{6}.$$

Sir Francis Bacon (1561-1626) authored the above quotation. He was an English philosopher, essayist, and statesman.

41

TETRAN

Can you fit all these pieces into the square below? All pieces must be used and none may overlap. Two have been placed for you.

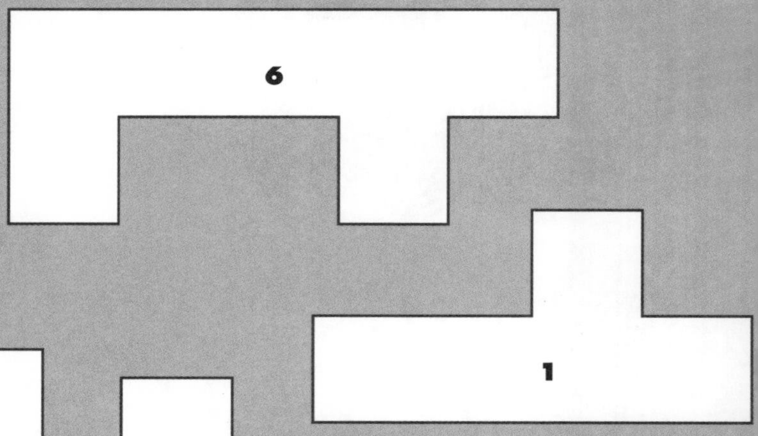

6

1

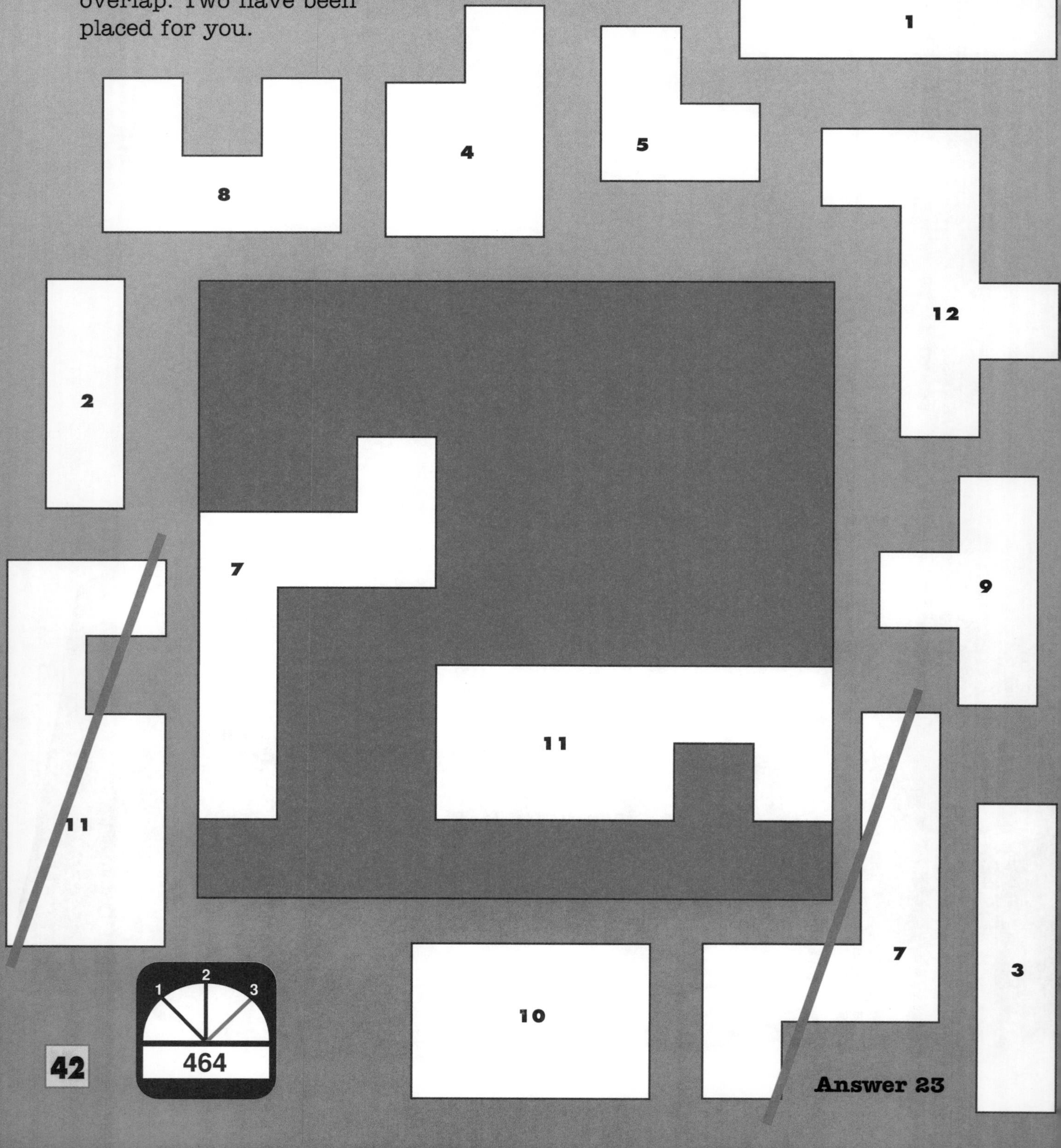

4

5

8

12

2

7

9

11

11

3

7

10

464

Answer 23

SCHEDULE SCRAMBLE

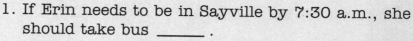

Can you use the posted schedule to answer Erin's questions? Once you've listed all the correct buses that leave from where Erin is now, read down the letters to find the answer to a riddle.

1. If Erin needs to be in Sayville by 7:30 a.m., she should take bus _____.
2. If Erin has to get to Skrantoon by 11:25 a.m., the last bus she can take is bus _____.
3. Erin wants to reach Las Venus by 10:50 a.m. The last bus she can take is bus _____.
4. To reach Pacific City before 10:30 a.m., the last bus is _____.
5. The first bus to reach Basilitia after 2:30 p.m. would be bus _____.
6. If Erin has to be in North Westly by 11:25 a.m., the last bus she can catch is bus _____.
7. The last bus into Coverton before 1:30 p.m. is bus _____.
8. To be in Bluffington before 8:00 a.m., the last bus to catch is bus _____.
9. The first bus to Barkly Hills after 3:00 p.m. is bus _____.
10. To be in Marville by 3:00 p.m., the last bus Erin can catch is bus _____.
11. The last bus of the day on this schedule is bus _____.

What did the spelling bee take to get to class?

LAKE HAVACARE

BUS STOP

575

BUS	A	B	C	H	L	O	S	U	Z
	A.M.								P.M.
Skrantoon	6:14	7:04	8:00	8:30	9:00	10:00	11:15	12:10	1:00
Bluffington	6:51	7:41	8:36	9:06	9:37	10:35	11:50	12:45	1:36
Sayville	7:20	8:10	9:07	9:37	10:07	11:06	12:22	1:15	2:07
North Westly	7:36	8:26	9:24	9:54	10:23	11:22	12:38	1:31	2:23
Pacific City	7:59	8:50	9:48	10:18	10:47	11:46	1:01	1:54	2:46
Marville	8:09	9:01	9:58	10:28	10:58	11:56	1:11	2:05	2:57
Las Venus	8:47	9:39	10:37	11:06	11:35	12:35	1:50	2:43	3:35
Barkly Hills	9:45	10:39	11:35	12:06	12:33	1:33	2:19	3:11	4:04
Coverton	10:10	11:05	12:00	12:30	12:57	1:57	2:45	3:54	4:40
Basilitia	11:00	11:58	12:55	1:21	1:46	2:44	3:35	4:44	5:28

Illustrated by Terry Kovalcik

ELECTRONIC READOUT

Some machines read information in binary code. Roughly, that means that the numeral 1 or the numeral 0 will appear and tell a machine whether to open or close its receptors. For the purposes of this puzzle, let's say that a 0 (zero) is closed and remains blank, while a 1 means the receptor is open and will fill with color.

The reason machines are so fast is that they read such coded information not just one number at a time but in a series. A series might look like this: 3 2 3 4 6 1, and so on. This would mean the first three blocks are blank, the second two are filled in, the next three are blank, the next four are filled in, and so on.

Each set of numbers below the grids tells how much of each grid to fill in. All numbers start in the upper left and go from left to right across the rows. Some filling in or blanks may continue from one row to the next. Every time a new number appears, it tells you to change to the opposite function as explained earlier. If the first number beneath the grid is not circled, start by filling in the blocks. If the first number is circled, start by leaving the blocks empty.

For example, let's try these two:

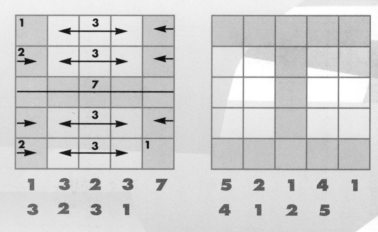

You should have spelled HI.

If everything is input correctly on the next page, you should find out who or what uses this type of code.

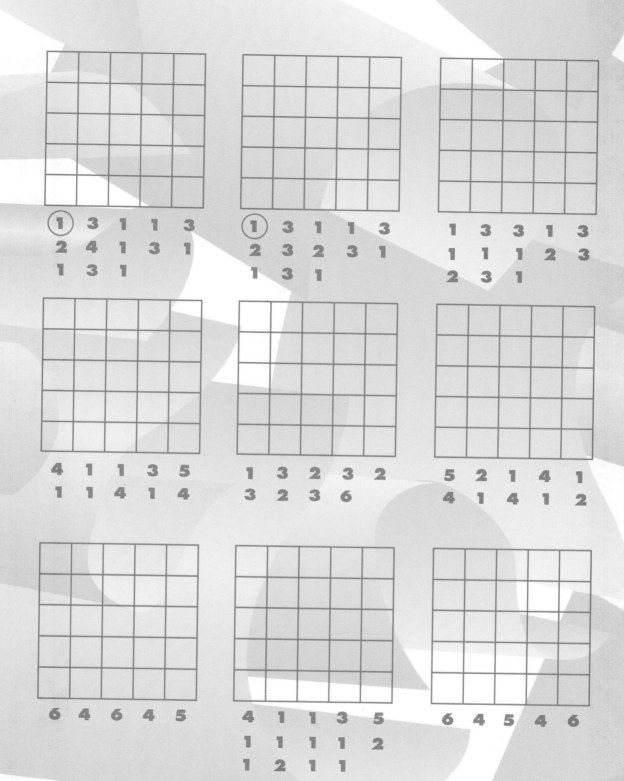

①	3	1	1	3
2	4	1	3	1
1	3	1		

①	3	1	1	3
2	3	2	3	1
1	3	1		

1	3	3	1	3
1	1	1	2	3
2	3	1		

4	1	1	3	5
1	1	4	1	4

1	3	2	3	2
3	2	3	6	

5	2	1	4	1
4	1	4	1	2

6	4	6	4	5

4	1	1	3	5
1	1	1	1	2
1	2	1	1	

6	4	5	4	6

686

MULTIPLE CHOICE

Forty-one different multiplication statements are hidden somewhere in this grid. They may be across, up, down, backward, or diagonal, and no number will appear in more than one equation. We've done two for you: 3 x 25 = 75 and 2 x 11 = 22. See if you can find the others.

3	4	12	75	25	3	6	48	10	4
8	6	10	1	1	1	24	5	3	4
1	46	7	40	8	2	2	4	30	16
8	46	6	42	9	50	6	25	6	1
3	1	54	7	72	8	5	9	2	18
24	9	22	7	48	5	3	7	21	8
6	11	3	49	6	6	36	5	3	8
2	4	16	3	9	2	10	20	9	64
12	8	9	7	63	9	3	9	27	45
2	27	4	1	4	18	81	10	4	40

What is the total if you multiply all the unused numbers going from left to right and top to bottom?

Answer 25

HINTS HINTS HINTS

102 I'M IN TROUBLE if you can't RISE ABOVE IT.

131 Statements 4, 10, and 20 are wrong.

133 Follow the arrows to get to the end.

201 If you can't guess the outer words, start at the center and build outward.

213 Think about what foods you might take on a picnic. Then scramble the letters and see if any of our words match yours.

242 In many cases, the initials of the words are used as the abbreviations.

244 You need 11 players for football, soccer, and cricket.

312 Sound it out! The animal in 9 is a ray.

324 D is the start. The next three are I, A, and K.

346 You're doing great!

353 Braille and Morse are the first two names you need.

355 If you leave for a moment, your napkin goes on your chair.

423 Both questions start with WHAT. One answer is A TEAR-IER.

435 You'll go nuts over this answer.

464 Keep moving the pieces around until you get a fit.

466 Only one number from 1 to 9 times itself will give you the same number.

511 Don't give up. Keep trying.

534 Of the three women, O'Connor tries, Earhart flies, and Sacajawea guides.

546 There may not be so many choices. The center is a good place to start.

561 Some tools may look like something other than what you'd expect. Look for nuts and bolts, too.

575 Bus A is the first one needed, while Z is the last bus needed.

577 The longest word will go into the longest set of boxes.

645 Don't CRAB as you grab the HELM and head the LIFEBOATS to the SEASHORES.

656 Only one nine-letter word and one six-letter word start with the same letter. See if you can sew those two together.

657 Look back at 656.

686 The first letter you should make is *C*.

688 If you don't know an answer on one grid, work back and forth using the letters on the other grid. All words begin in a numbered box, but they may go off in unusual directions.

756 Cobblers make shoes. Coopers make barrels.

768 Tinothy has the most arms. Cy has the fewest eyes.

797 The three numbers in any group should equal a *multiplication* equation. You need to imagine that the symbols are there.

799 Try different letters until you find ones that will help make words.

802 *Flora* is a word for plants, Alberta is in Canada, and *Martha* is a woman's name.

867 Some people eat these with mustard.

879 You'll turn green if you can't get these answers.

978 Not all eggs come from chickens.

980 The wet woman will get off first. One man just pressed for the fourth floor.

982 That's all, folks.

ANSWERS

1. SEW SIMPLE (pages 10-11)

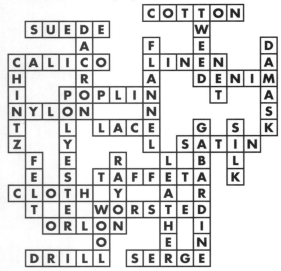

SuperChallenge: Cotton is a natural fiber. The others are all man-made.

2. TOOLS OF THE TRADE (page 22)

Cobbler—G   Cooper—C   Orthodontist—A
Photographer—F   Glazier—B   Surveyor—E
Ophthalmologist—D

3. TEAM SPIRIT (page 27)

Football—11	Baseball—9
Basketball—5	Soccer—11
Hockey—6	Polo—4
Rugby—13	Cricket—11
Lacrosse—10	Bowling—4
Volleyball—6	Relay Race—4

The total number of players is 94.

SuperChallenge: Half of 94 is 47. Here is our answer. You may have found another combination that works as well. One column should have the following teams:

Polo, Bowling, or Relay Race	4
Rugby	13
Football, Soccer, or Cricket	11
Baseball	9
Lacrosse	+10
	47

The remaining teams go into the second column.

4. WILD WORDS (page 4)

1. I'm in trouble	6. Split ends
2. Rise above it	7. I understand
3. Button up	8. Thank-you note
4. Milk shake	9. TV star
5. Double cross	

SuperChallenge: Put on your long underwear and overcoat.

5. PLANTING ROWS (page 15)

CARROTS
COSTAR
ROAST
STAR
TAR
AT
A
AN
NAG
RANG
ORGAN
GROANS
ORANGES

SuperChallenge: 1. Carrots and oranges are both orange in color. 2. soar, oars

6. DUPLI-GRIDS (pages 32-33)

SuperChallenge: Twine

7. ADD IT UP (page 30)

9	3	7
6	2	5
4	8	1

$1 \times 1 = 1$

$1 + 1 = 2$

$4 + 3 = 7$

$1 + 2 = 3$

$2 \times 4 = 8$

$2 \times 2 = 4$

$2 + 2 + 2 = 6$

$3 \times 3 = 9$

$4 + 1 = 5$

8. I WAS THE FIRST (page 19)
1. John Hancock
2. Edmund Halley
3. Marco Polo
4. George Washington Carver
5. Amelia Earhart
6. Clarence Birdseye
7. Yuri Gagarin
8. Neil Armstrong
9. Sacajawea
10. Roger Bannister

SuperChallenge: Sandra Day O'Connor, Jackie Robinson

9. WHAT AM I? (page 8)
I am a squirrel.

SuperChallenge: Antarctica

10. IF . . . THEN (pages 36-37)
"Imagination is more important than knowledge."
— Albert Einstein

11. TWISTED LOGIC (page 23)
Snack: Pretzel

SuperChallenge: Germany

12. RAIN-FOREST RESCUE (pages 6-7)
D, I, A, K, E, F, J, H, C, B, L, G

13. THREE IS A MATCH (page 35)
1. Parts of a cap: Bill Strap Crown
2. Names for money: Buck Cash Fin
3. Bosses: Foreman Manager Supervisor
4. Names of deer: Stag Fawn Doe
5. Canadian Provinces: Alberta Manitoba Ontario
6. People named George: Washington Bush Burns
7. American States: Colorado Utah Ohio
8. Female names: Virginia Martha Georgia
9. Names for plants: Tree Flora Shrub
10. Parts of a fish: Scale Gill Tail

14. SCHEDULE SCRAMBLE (page 43)
1. A 2. S 3. C 4. H 5. O 6. O 7. L
8. B 9. U 10. Z 11. Z

What did the spelling bee take to get to class?
SCHOOL BUZZ

15. ARROW HEADINGS (page 26)

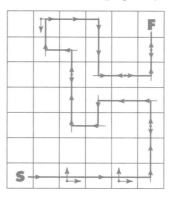

16. WORD STRIPS (page 13)
1. thumbs
2. sleeves
3. artichokes
4. unripe bananas
5. pine trees
6. shamrocks

SuperChallenge: These are all green things.

17. COVER

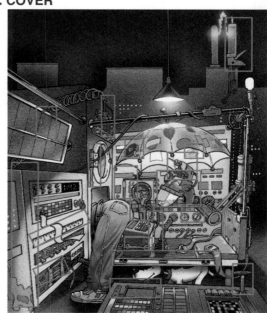

18. SPARE PARTS (pages 16-17)
1. Steering wheel
2. Passenger door
3. Glove compartment
4. Windshield wiper
5. Jack
6. Grill
7. Headlight
8. Spare tire
9. Radiator

SuperChallenge: Battery cable

19. SHOPPING LIST (page 34)

1. **T** ar **T**
  O le **O**
  P um **P**

2. **C** omi **C**
  R efe **R**
  A lph **A**
  Y olk **Y**
  O utg **O**
  N ylo **N**
  S kie **S**

3. **T** igh **T**
  E ras **E**
  D rie **D**
  D rea **D**
  Y umm **Y**
  B lur **B**
  E vad **E**
  A rom **A**
  R umo **R**

4. **S** pie **S**
  K aya **K**
  A rom **A**
  T rea **T**
  E agl **E**
  B lur **B**
  O utg **O**
  A ren **A**
  R ive **R**
  D rie **D**

20. SHORT STUFF (pages 38-39)

21. GOING UP (page 14)

Miss Timmons—6th floor
Mrs. Olsen—5th floor
Mr. Burns—4th floor
Mr. Lang—3rd floor
Ms. Murphy—2nd floor

   SuperChallenge: A. Lang B. Timmons C. Burns
D. Olsen E. Murphy

22. KNOT LIKELY (page 31)

   SuperChallenge: You might also find a knot in wood, on your head, or in your stomach. A knot you can't see is at sea. A knot is a unit that measures the speed of a ship.

23. TETRAN (page 42)

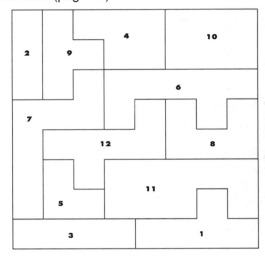

24. EGGSCRUCIATING (pages 24-25)

1. WHY WAS THE ROOSTER SO SHY?
   HE LED A SHELL-TERED LIFE.

2. WHY DID HUMPTY DUMPTY HAVE A GREAT FALL?
   TO MAKE UP FOR A BAD SUMMER.

3. WHAT BIRD SHOULD YOU THINK OF WHEN AN EGG
   IS THROWN AT YOU? DUCK!

   SuperChallenge: Here are six creatures that are hatched from eggs: snake, turtle, bird, fish, sea horse, and platypus. You may have found others, including frog, spider, and lizard.

25. MULTIPLE CHOICE (page 46)

3	4	12	75	25	3	6	48	10	4
8	6	10	1	1	1	24	5	3	4
1	46	7	40	8	2	2	4	30	16
8	46	6	42	9	50	6	25	6	1
3	1	54	7	72	8	5	9	2	18
24	9	22	7	48	5	3	7	21	8
6	11	3	49	6	6	36	5	3	8
2	4	16	3	9	2	10	20	9	64
12	8	9	7	63	9	3	9	27	45
2	27	4	1	4	18	81	10	4	40

SuperChallenge: 6 X 50 = 300; 1 X 300 = 300

26. 'BOT-Y BUILDER (page 12)

A. Cy   C. Gearheart
B. Tinothy   D. Micah-chip